Guinea Pigs

AUTHOR: IMMANUEL BIRMELIN | PHOTOGRAPHER: OLIVER GIEL

Contents

More Than Meets the Eye

Guinea pigs often have the reputation of being boring and even a little stupid, yet quite the opposite is true. Not only do the little rodents have an exciting behavioral repertoire, but they are also extremely curious and adept at learning, provided they are given the proper encouragement.

On the Trail of the Guinea Pig

Guinea pigs are among the oldest domestic animals in South America. The Indians began keeping them more than 4,000 years ago, and even today the plump little creatures remain one of their favorite dishes. They are sold in the markets of every small village, and buyers haggle loudly over the price, which is determined by weight and the quality of the meat. The guinea pigs' appearance has been altered by humankind over the centuries, but it still reveals something about their wild ancestors. The Wild Cavy (*Cavia aperea*), the forebear of our present-day guinea pig, survives and can be found inhabiting the temperate regions of South America. It is more slender, smaller, and uniformly dark grayish brown in color. This coat color helps it blend in perfectly with its surroundings. Camouflage and speed ensure the survival of the Wild Cavy in its rugged natural habitat. It becomes active at dusk and scurries along well-worn trails from burrow to burrow. Like our domestic guinea pigs, it lives in colonies; usually one male rules a harem of several females. In contrast to our pet guinea pigs, though, Wild Cavies can bite when threatened.

How did guinea pigs make their way from South America to Europe? The Spanish conquerors brought them to Europe in the sixteenth century. No one is really sure whether they used the animals as a source of meat during the crossing or if they simply took a fancy to the little critters. What's certain is that the animals were not used for food in Europe. These beloved rodents owe their popularity to their temperament and appearance. They are friendly, easy to tame, like to be around people, and, at first glance, are simple to care for.

Guinea Pig Behavior

If you love your guinea pigs and want to keep them properly, you have to understand something about their behavior. You should know how they communicate with each other and what individual signals mean. Guinea pigs use body language and vocalizations to let their herd mates know exactly what they want. Their message is easy for us humans to understand. Here is a little dictionary of "guinea pig language."

Freezing: The word describes exactly how guinea pigs behave when they are startled or frightened.

Ever watchful, the guinea pig stands up to get a better view. There's something new here.

They stand perfectly still, as though turned to stone, and all movement is, so to speak, "frozen."

Threatening: Before males start to fight, they try to intimidate each other with threat displays. Perhaps one of the adversaries will give up and unnecessary bloodshed will be avoided. This behavior makes sense biologically. The males try to impress each other by presenting their flanks and ruffling up their hair. This display is accompanied by loud tooth chattering and lowering of their testicles. The opponents circle each other while "purring" and making long-drawn-out "grrr" sounds. Threatening behavior is rarely observed in females.

Treading: This behavior is often displayed along with threatening. When treading, the guinea pig places more weight on his front legs and lifts first one hind leg and then the other. His rump sways back and forth. Treading is observed primarily in subordinate animals.

Yawning: This is a submissive gesture and means that the loser of a fight would like to concede. It has nothing to do with feeling sleepy.

Rumba: The male courts the female with these dance-like movements. He approaches the female and struts around her in slow motion, all the while shifting his body weight from one leg to the other. He announces his intentions with "purring" sounds.

Urine spraying: This is an unusual method of rebuffing a suitor. If the male is too pushy, the

These two guinea pigs know each other. To be on the safe side, though, they sniff each other carefully to make sure they really belong to the same family.

Guinea pigs find strength in numbers. Today we know that the animals can handle stress much better if they live together with others of their kind.

female sprays him with urine. She can send a jet of urine a distance of almost 12 inches (30 cm).

Jumping: Like high-spirited children, guinea pigs, especially young ones, jump straight up into the air from a standing position. Called "popcorning," it is an expression of playful exuberance that other youngsters find catching.

Squealing: This is a begging sound—a long, penetrating whistle that the animal uses to beg for food. Rarely does a "well-trained" guinea pig owner ignore this call for help.

Screaming: When guinea pigs are afraid or in pain, they scream. It sounds like a long-drawn-out shriek.

Whining: This sound is unmistakable. It is a long, soft, high-pitched cry and arouses sympathy. Guinea pigs whine when they are alone and unhappy.

Purring: Males purr during courtship and when threatening. It is a deep sound with trills.

Guinea pigs need partners

As you can see, guinea pigs are fascinating animals with an extensive vocabulary and a wide range of expressive behaviors at their disposal. Detecting and observing this is possible only if you keep more than one animal. Guinea pigs are herd animals. Sociability is inscribed in their genes. How they get along with each other, though, depends on their personal experience—in other words, how they were raised. Early development and puberty are especially important for males. That's when they learn how to deal with their position in the herd later on. The older males in the herd are "sparring partners." Males that grew up alone, without partners of the same sex, have problems getting along in the herd. They never learned the rules of the colony and are bullied or become troublemakers. The females have an easier time achieving their rank in a new herd, regardless of how they spent their youth.

Who Will Get Along Together?

Although guinea pigs are herd animals and should never be kept singly, not every animal fits in with every group; that's because, as with us humans, there are easygoing as well as aggressive types. So who will get along with whom?

Keeping females: For the most part, female guinea pigs get along well together. Although they do quarrel on occasion, this squabbling usually subsides quickly. However, aggression in a group like this is somewhat greater than in a herd with one male and several females.

Keeping males: I advise against keeping several adult males, because there is too great a danger that the animals will bite each other. There are fewer problems if you keep only two males.

Many guinea pig owners have been successful with this approach. This presupposes, however, that the cage is large and the animals can avoid each other if they want to. If they still keep fighting, you should separate them. An older and a younger male usually get along best because the "old man" is the undisputed boss.

Keeping a group: The ideal guinea pig group consists of several males and several females. Each member of the group knows the rules, which keeps the level of aggression low. Conflict is preprogrammed in a herd where there are just a few males and many females, because the males will fight over the females.

Strength in numbers

Guinea pigs are very susceptible to stress. Like us humans, they have so-called stress hormones. These hormones (for example, cortisol) are found in the blood and are produced in glands. If an animal is afraid or feels threatened, the level of stress hormones in his blood increases. This increase is an unmistakable sign of stress. Stress isn't always bad, though; it causes illness only when it persists for a long time and cannot be alleviated. If a solitary guinea pig is taken from familiar surroundings and placed all alone in a sparsely furnished cage, his stress-hormone level rises perceptibly. When the same experiment was carried out with two animals, the results were surprising. In the sparsely furnished cage, the levels of stress hormones in both animals were distinctly lower. The guinea pig's heart, which weighs just 1/16 ounce (2.1 g), also is affected when he

This little rascal is just seven days old and is already eating like the grown-ups. Guinea pigs are fully developed at birth.

Cork tubes are ideal in the outdoor enclosure. As you can see, each of the three guinea pigs has found a favorite spot. Cork tubes are fun to run through, and they make great lookouts. The natural material is very comfortable for little paws, too.

is tense: His heart rate speeds up. Normally the heart beats 230 times a minute, but under stress it pounds even faster. What a performance when compared with the human heart (50 to 80 beats a minute)! In a solitary guinea pig, this agitated state lasts 30 minutes. If there are two animals, the heart begins to beat normally after just three minutes. These figures demonstrate clearly just how important a partner is for guinea pigs. They find strength in numbers.

Rabbits and Guinea Pigs

Although it's true that guinea pigs and rabbits tolerate each other, they do not communicate the way members of the same species do. Rabbits and guinea pigs "speak" different languages, and they also have different circadian rhythms.

Anatomy and Senses

Teeth

The teeth grow through-out life; cheek teeth (molars and premolars) can grow up to 1/16 inch (1.5 mm) a week. It's easy to calculate how long the teeth would be after two years if they weren't worn down by chewing on hard materi-als like twigs.

Tongue

The tongue performs many functions. It is used for eating, helps with swallowing and grooming, and has an impressive number of taste buds. Guinea pigs prefer foods that are slightly—but not too—sweet. They don't like bitter foods.

Feet

Each front foot has four toes and each hind foot has three. Guinea pigs have sweat glands and sebaceous glands on the pads of their feet. They must be able to wear down their toenails on a hard floor. Overgrown nails should be trimmed, preferably by a veterinarian, because they can cause pain when the animal walks.

Coat

Wild Cavies have an inconspic-uous grayish brown coat of hair. This is important in the wild so that the animals avoid attracting the attention of their numerous enemies. Our modern domestic guinea pigs, on the other hand, have coats that come in many different colors, lengths, and textures.

Eyes

The eyes are on either side of the head. Advantage: Enemies cannot approach unnoticed from behind. The price for this: Depth perception is not very good. Guinea pigs probably see colors as well as we do.

Nose

Smell plays a major role in a guinea pig's life. It helps the animal communicate and identify others of his kind. A guinea pig learns to recognize you by your personal scent, which is why your hands shouldn't smell like perfume, cleaning products, or your dog. Tactile hairs (whiskers), arranged around the mouth, are especially useful in the dark. They help the guinea pig find his way. When the tactile hairs brush against an object, this gives the animal needed information.

Ears

Guinea pigs hear very well. They recognize each other by individual sounds and communicate by cooing and chattering. The animals are especially sensitive to high-frequency noise.

Why solitude is unhealthy

Without a partner, a guinea pig's life is lonely and boring. There is no one to talk to or play with. Guinea pigs that were removed from their group when young and forced to live alone exhibit severe behavioral problems. Reintroducing a guinea pig like this to an intact herd causes difficulties as well.

If animals that were kept alone for more than a year, starting at two months of age, are then put into an intact group, they have trouble getting along. Many of them die without ever getting involved in a fight. Unfortunately, you can't tell that they're suffering from potentially fatal stress by looking at them. Those that survive lose almost 20 percent of their weight within a few weeks and have a lower rank in the group. Naturally, these important scientific findings are of significance for every responsible pet owner. They teach us, on the one hand, how necessary the guinea pig's partner is and, on the other hand, that guinea pigs cannot simply be housed together haphazardly.

Today we also know that when female guinea pigs are frequently placed in a new herd and thus keep meeting new animals, they gain weight because of anxiety. Their hormones reveal that they are suffering from stress. Just like humans, they eat out of frustration. The stress, however, has no effect on the number of their offspring. They have as many young as females that always live in the same herd. Unfortunately, females that "wander" from herd to herd do not live as long as those that stay in a stable herd. As we have come to understand, the group life of these little rodents is very complex. Who would have thought it?

Children and guinea pigs are perfect together. Nevertheless, kids still need parental supervision and guidance when it comes to handling their pets.

Children and Guinea Pigs

RESPECT Teach your children consideration, respect, and love for the animals.

PROPER TREATMENT Show your children how they must treat their guinea pigs.

CARE Make sure that the guinea pigs are fed regularly and that their cage is clean.

TRUST Guinea pigs easily form a bond with their little friends and become tame relatively quickly.

HARMLESS Guinea pigs do not bite or defend themselves; instead, they run away when they've had enough.

A Day in the Life of a Guinea Pig

The actors in this case are my guinea pigs. There is Barny, the boss; Castry, the castrated male; and the two females, Mona and Lisa. I spent several days and nights observing the life of these four animals and recording them with a video camera. I have a very personal relationship with each of my guinea pigs. They know me well, respond to their names, and greet me every day with friendly squeals.

When observing my little herd, I frequently noticed that guinea pigs never lick or groom each other the way many other animals, such as rabbits, do. Social grooming plays no role in the life of a guinea pig. That doesn't mean that it's boring to watch them, though. Given the opportunity, guinea pigs love to go exploring and learn quickly.

The guinea pig's day begins early. At daybreak they set out on their search for food and inspect their pen noisily. It turns out that they're regular little "chatterboxes." With eyes and nose, they carefully examine every new thing. After their lengthy excursion, they take a break. What happens next depends on how the cage is furnished (page 22). If the setup is interesting, they happily make use of what's there.

During the day, there are five to seven lengthy periods of activity, followed by times of rest. Animals who like each other nap together. Castry was especially remarkable. He was always exploring and was also the star pupil in our learning trials. There was little squabbling within the group. At night the guinea pigs usually slept. Between two and three in the morning, however, they were quite active.

This blanket smells like the guinea pig's family, and that makes him feel safe and secure. It's also a great place for snuggling and hiding.

Guidelines for Happiness

TIPS FROM
GUINEA PIG EXPERT
Immanuel Birmelin

GUINEA PIG PALS: We don't know if animals experience happiness, but we do know that they can feel contented. Guinea pigs definitely need others of their kind. There should be at least two guinea pigs; with each addition to the group, you have to think carefully about who will get along with whom (page 8).

SPACE: The cage shouldn't be too small, otherwise the sensitive little creatures will become apathetic and lazy (page 22).

FURNISHINGS: Cage and pen must be designed so they are guinea pig friendly and provide plenty of variety (pages 23 and 24).

DIET: Guinea pigs love to eat. A balanced diet keeps them healthy (page 39).

ACTIVITIES: Daily out-of-cage time indoors and visits to the outdoor enclosure improve their well-being. Guinea pigs are always ready for "mental exercise" and learning little tricks, too (page 54).

Be sure before you buy

Don't let yourself be led astray when buying guinea pigs; instead, ask yourself and your children if you are all ready to take on the work involved in caring for these cute little rodents. And very important: You should be fairly certain that you will keep the animals for the rest of their life. Changing owners frequently is bad for guinea pigs. They are sensitive little creatures and get used to you and their surroundings. It is not easy for guinea pigs to become trusting. That's why I urge you not to be hasty when deciding to make a purchase. Before you get the animals, check to see if you are allergic to guinea pig hair or the cage bedding. Consider, too, how other pets, like birds, dogs, or cats, may react to the new family members. It's relatively easy to get well-trained dogs or birds to accept guinea pigs. Cats are more difficult, because many cats regard guinea pigs as prey, and no one can convince them otherwise. In addition, think about what you'll do with the animals during your vacation (page 58).

Where to find guinea pigs

You can get guinea pigs at a pet store, from a breeder, from private individuals, or at an animal shelter. Which you prefer depends on your confidence in the seller. When making your selection, though, pay attention to the following points:
›   The cage must be large and clean. A thick layer of small animal bedding is essential for keeping guinea pigs.
›   Ventilation must be good.
›   Water and a hay rack must be available in the cage.
›   It's important to give them twigs and branches to chew on.
›   In a large herd, the animals need several hide boxes.

> Guinea pigs should not live alone. Rabbits are no substitute for other guinea pigs, but they can be kept together with a herd of guinea pigs.

> Ask the seller about the age of the animals and where they come from. If the guinea pigs have traveled a long distance, possibly in small cages, there's a danger that they may have experienced a shock and will be harder to tame.

How old?

If you are a novice guinea pig owner, then I suggest you get young animals. Six to eight weeks is a good age. At this age, they are still easy to tell apart from full-grown animals. Although they look like adults, they are clearly smaller and weigh less. If all the dealer's animals are the same size, then ask him or her to weigh your favorite. It shouldn't weigh more than 12 ounces (350 g). This way you can be fairly certain that it's a youngster.

How to determine the sex

It is not very difficult to determine the sex of a guinea pig, even for a novice, despite the fact that the male's penis lies hidden in a fold of abdominal skin. However, a little trick unambiguously reveals which you've got—a male or a female. Hold the

The little rodents are crazy about this fabric tunnel with different entrances and exits. If they decide to chew on it, though, this "luxury" won't last long.

15

animal on its back and with your finger gently press its belly near the anus. In males, the penis will protrude. In females, the genital region looks like the letter Y. The distance between anal and genital openings is smaller in females than in males (photos, below).

Siblings get along

Try to buy two or three siblings at the same time, because then the animals know each other and are already friends. This prevents aggression, helps them overcome their initial shyness in new surroundings more quickly, and makes them easier

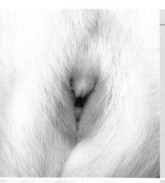

1 Determining the sex is quite easy with guinea pigs. In young females, the genital opening looks like the letter Y.

2 When you press gently on the anal region of a male's belly, the little penis protrudes distinctly. This is easy to recognize, even for a novice.

to tame. Of course, finding siblings is a matter of luck, especially in a pet store, but you can often get youngsters that are living in a herd. Don't make the mistake of buying just one animal initially in the hope of being able to tame it more easily. Although this is true of many animals, it is not the case with guinea pigs. They do better in a group, and then they will quickly become trusting. A small group of two or three guinea pigs is a good choice (page 8).

Tip: If you would like to provide a home for older animals—from an animal shelter, for instance—there is basically nothing to prevent you from doing so. It may just take a little longer for you to win the animals' trust.

Castration: If males and females live in the herd, it is necessary to prevent offspring (page 32). The only option here is castration. Unfortunately there is no contraceptive pill for guinea pigs like there is for lions and tigers. For the guinea pig itself, neutering is a drastic intervention. The removal of ovaries or testicles changes the behavior of the animals. Males stop producing the male hormone testosterone, and quarrelsome roughnecks can turn into peaceful members of the herd. Females tend to put on weight.

Tip: I advise against neutering females, because it is riskier and more difficult medically than for males.

Sometimes it's hard to decide

If you're faced with an adorable passel of guinea pigs, which of the lively little rascals should you choose? Would you rather have a purebred variety or an ordinary domestic guinea pig? This is a question only you can answer. I prefer the "normal" domestic guinea pig, one without excessively long hair (Breed portraits, pages 18/19). Very long hair is difficult to care for and interferes with the animal's ability to see. Perhaps that's why long-haired guinea pigs are less active than guinea pigs with normal-length hair. The criteria I use when making my decision are the health and behavior of the guinea pig (Checklist, right). Evaluating behavior is no simple task, so here's a tip: Don't buy the animals on your first visit; instead, take a look at the group at least twice. It's easy to understand why. Guinea pigs have a circadian rhythm, just like us humans. If you happen to observe the animals during a period when they're sleeping, you might get the wrong impression of them.

Behavior test: This little test will tell you a lot about the guinea pigs you're thinking of buying. Ask the salesperson to reach into the cage as if to catch one of the animals. Now it gets interesting: If the guinea pigs run for the safety of their hide box, that's good and perfectly normal. After a few minutes, though, curiosity should get the better of their fear. The guinea pigs should stick their noses out of the box and have a look around to see what's up. However, if one of the animals just sits there without budging, he might have behavioral problems, or he could be sick.

Health at a Glance

CHECK	PAY ATTENTION TO
BEHAVIOR	To make sure you are not seeing the animals only during a rest period, visit them more than once and at different times of the day. Carry out the behavior test (text, left below).
GAIT	Does the guinea pig move normally and put weight on his limbs evenly without limping?
FEET	Are the feet positioned correctly, and are the toenails straight?
TEETH	Are the teeth healthy? The incisors should be of equal length, and the cheek teeth should not be visibly misaligned.
EYES	Are the eyes clear and free of discharge?
EARS	Are the ears clean, without waxy buildup or crusty areas?
NOSE	Is the nose pink, dry, and free of discharge?
COAT	Is the coat shiny, with no bald spots or parasites?
ANUS	Is the anus clean and not caked with dirt? Are there any traces of diarrhea?
SKIN	Is the skin free of scars and scabs?

Guinea Pig Portraits

Today's colorful domestic guinea pigs are quite different from their inconspicuous wild ancestors with their grayish brown coats. Here is a small selection of the most popular breeds and varieties.

WHITE CRESTED: The unique feature of this breed is the crest. Here are a chocolate animal and a cream-colored one.

SATIN: Their coat is especially fine and lustrous. The distinctive sheen is caused by the fact that the hair shaft is hollow, which makes it reflect light differently. Satin guinea pigs are considered to be somewhat skittish. This little fellow has a red coat.

SILVER AGOUTI: In these guinea pigs, the hairs of the undercoat are dark at the base and light at the tip. This gives the short, easy-care coat a wonderful "silvery" luster.

ABYSSINIAN: Tricolor Abyssinian guinea pigs are very popular. The whorls of hair ("rosettes") give the little rascals a comical appearance.

PERUVIAN: They have long hair, two rosettes on the rump and one on the head, a part down the middle of the back, and long bangs (called the "frontal"). This one is black and white.

ENGLISH SELF-CRESTED: Although these animals have a crest, it is the same color as the coat, not white as in the White Crested. Here is one with a red crest.

MARKED: This black-and-white marked guinea pig is very pretty. The smooth coat needs very little care and does not get dirty easily.

Welcome Home

At last—the moment you've been waiting for: The guinea pigs are moving in! You've finished setting up the cage and placed it in the right spot. Now the animals can take their time exploring their new home. Make your guinea pigs feel right at home by speaking gently to them and tempting them with little treats.

Guinea Pigs Feel Right at Home Here

Each of us knows how important it is to make our house feel like a home. This pleasant feeling is important for our emotional and physical well-being. It's not much different with animals. They also need a place of safety and refuge. What constitutes appropriate housing for an animal varies from species to species. Some pets might need lots of room; others require specific temperatures and lighting conditions. Fortunately, guinea pigs are not very demanding. With a little know-how you can give them comfortable quarters that meet their requirements. Nevertheless, you still have to know the best location for the cage, how large it should be, and how you can furnish it so that it's both practical and entertaining for your guinea pigs. That's a lot of questions, but let's take them in order.

The right location

Never put the cage in direct sunlight, because the guinea pigs could suffer a fatal heatstroke there. Instead, choose a place that offers both sun and shade. A bright room with moderate temperature is best. Temperatures between 59 and 68°F (15 and 20°C) are ideal. Guinea pigs can tolerate slight variations, though. Drafts are very bad for guinea pigs. Noises don't disturb them much, provided the sounds are not too high-pitched. High-frequency sounds make the animals panic. It's a good idea to place the cage on a small table. The advantage of this is that you can watch the guinea pigs more comfortably at eye level, and the little rodents are protected from unpleasant surprises like the dog's nose. Ultimately, though, it's a matter of personal preference.

The cage: A place of safety and security

Guinea pigs are lively creatures and very active during the day. That's why your motto should be "the bigger the cage, the better." Sometimes this isn't possible, though, because your house is too small. In order to satisfy the guinea pigs' thirst for activity, you should make their cage interesting and provide some time every day for the animals to go exploring either indoors or out (page 26).

Minimum size: For two guinea pigs the cage should be at least 48 inches (120 cm) long, 32 inches (80 cm) wide, and 18 inches (45 cm) high.

Cage design: The cages in a pet store consist of a bottom tray and a wire top. The plastic tray should be a maximum of 6 inches (15 cm) deep so that the animals can see what's going on outside. This protects them from any unwelcome surprises, prevents stress and panic, and reduces the buildup of heat and unpleasant odors. Here's a tip: Buy a cage with horizontal galvanized wires. That way your inquisitive pets can stand on their hind legs by resting their front feet on the wires and then watch what's going on outside the cage.

Tip: Connecting two or more smaller cages is an ideal way to increase the floor space. The advantage of this is that the cages are not so cumbersome and can be moved around more easily. You can even join the cages around a corner. There are many possibilities. The guinea pigs will reward your efforts with increased curiosity.

For some time, pet stores have been selling multilevel condo cages for guinea pigs—also a good solution. Make sure, though, that the ramps to the upper level are made of wood. Plastic is not suitable for guinea pig feet.

When spending even a few hours in their outdoor pen, the animals need a hide box where they feel safe and secure.

Tips for Preventing Boredom

MOVE THE CAGE: From time to time, move the cage to another spot in the room. This has a tremendous effect on the guinea pigs.

A DIFFERENT PERSPECTIVE: The guinea pigs will now see the room from a new vantage point; if you move the cage to a different room, even the smells will be new.

NEW IMPRESSIONS: These new sensory impressions counteract boredom. The animals now have a new view of their surroundings but still feel safe and secure in their familiar cage. Guinea pigs that break out of their daily routine are much more inquisitive.

Cage bedding: I cover the floor of the cage with a layer of wood shavings about 4 to 6 inches (10 to 15 cm) deep; this is available at pet stores. Garden peat and cat litter are not suitable as cage bedding for guinea pigs.

A hide box for all

Guinea pigs are herd animals and seek contact with each other. That's why I recommend a hide box that has plenty of room for all. This helps them feel like part of the group and gives the individual animals a sense of security. Sometimes, though, guinea pigs, like people, just want to be alone. Although that's not very common, it does happen occasionally. For times like these I provide my animals with a one-pig apartment. However, a second hide box is practical only if the cage is large enough.

Decorating with style: This idea comes from Ms. Zopfi-Fischli of the University of Bern (Switzerland). She designed cages with movable wooden partitions of different sizes. By moving the walls, a cage like this can easily be rearranged. The results were amazing. The guinea pigs became more lively, and subordinate animals were able to avoid their rivals.

Adventure indoors

Guinea pigs love to go exploring indoors. Unfortunately, all sorts of dangers lie in wait for the little rodents here (Checklist, page 55). In addition, most guinea pigs are not house-trained and leave their droppings wherever they happen to be at the moment. So here's my tip: Buy a collapsible exercise pen at the pet store and set it up next to the cage. To protect the floor of your room, lay down a heavy plastic sheet (pond liner) in the pen and cover it with a layer of newspaper to soak up the urine. As the top layer, use a chewable woven grass mat. Carpet remnants without loops will serve the purpose, too. The advantage of a pen is that the animals are safe and there's less cleanup for you.

When you hand-feed your guinea pig treats, she will come to see you as a bearer of goodies. This helps build trust.

The Guinea Pig Home

Hay rack

The daily hay ration shouldn't just be scattered on the floor of the cage, but should be offered in a food rack. This way the hay won't be contaminated by feces and urine. Racks that hang on the outside of the cage take up less space.

Water bottles

Fresh water must always be readily available to the guinea pigs. A sipper bottle keeps it clean. Of course, sipper bottles can also spread germs if they are not cleaned thoroughly. Make it a rule, then, to wash the bottles daily with hot water.

Bowls

Food bowls must be tip-proof. Bowls made of ceramic or stoneware are best. For full-grown animals, bowls with a high rim that curves inward are practical. Smaller animals need a shallower food dish. Always use separate bowls for fresh and dry foods.

House

A hide box in the cage or pen should be roomy enough for all your guinea pigs. They'll enjoy snuggling inside; an animal can also retreat there if she's not in the mood for company.

Food ball

Activity is very important for guinea pigs. That's why in many modern zoos the animals have to "work" for their food, just as they do in the wild. There is a wide range of possibilities for guinea pigs. The food ball pictured here can be filled with hay or fresh foods and hung in the cage. You can build a "food tree" like the one in the photo on page 41 or spread around treats such as bits of carrot.

Cork tubes

Cork tubes are wonderfully versatile. They can be joined together in all possible combinations, and you can even put one inside the other. Your guinea pigs can enjoy the view from on top and can also nibble on them. They make great hiding places, too.

Outdoor "Playground"

All animals love to be outdoors. Fresh air, sun, and even a bit of rain increase their resistance to disease and sharpen their senses. They are no different from us in this respect. Every physician recommends walks and fresh air. So take the little rodents outdoors whenever possible. A yard is ideal, naturally, but a balcony will do, too. Out in the yard the guinea pigs can romp around and discover new things. That strengthens their muscles and stimulates their curiosity. Boredom, the bane of so many pets, never has a chance to develop outdoors. Boredom, by the way, is a serious problem for pets, causing many of them to become apathetic or develop behavioral problems.

But back to the "fresh air oasis." How much sun, rain, and wind can a guinea pig take? The little rodents have no problem coping with small amounts of sun, rain, and wind. Naturally they shouldn't be out in the soaking rain for hours or exposed to constant wind and excessive heat (The right location, page 21). Just think about how you would feel, assuming you're not a fresh-air fanatic or outdoorsy type. Guinea pigs enjoy things in small doses, and that applies to their surroundings and new experiences. A mixture of the normal and the novel is just right. Guinea pigs need familiar reference points, like their hideaway or a partition with their scent.

A little natural paradise

What should this kind of outdoor enclosure for a guinea pig look like? Safety for the defenseless animals is the first requirement. Pet stores sell movable outdoor pens. They consist of folding wire panels with a net stretched over the top. Of course, these pens can be used to house the animals only for a few hours under supervision. There is too great a danger that a cat or dog will wander into the yard and destroy the net with its claws or nose.

An indoor enclosure attached directly to the opened cage lets the animals move around and enjoy a change of scenery.

Guinea pigs can live on the balcony if it is large enough, well protected, and has a weatherproof shelter.

This movable outdoor pen made of wire panels is available at pet stores. It is perfect for letting your guinea pigs spend a few hours outdoors.

Outdoor enclosures that are intruder-proof and solid yet movable are also available at pet stores. The sturdy wire walls, wire roof, and shelter (hide box) form a unit. The only disadvantage: They are not especially large (6-1/2 feet [2 m] long, and 20 inches [50 cm] wide).

Do-it-yourself: If you are good with your hands, you can build your guinea pigs an outdoor enclosure using simple materials. But how large should this natural paradise be? The saying "the bigger the better" applies here, too. My little guinea pig herd has an outdoor enclosure measuring 6-1/2 × 5 feet (2 × 1.5 m). To build it yourself, you need wood lath and wire mesh. Make sure that the openings in the mesh aren't too large so that neither guinea pigs nor rats and other predators can squeeze through. Use the wood lath to build the individual frames, which should be between 12 and 16 inches (30 and 40 cm) high. The wire mesh is stretched over the frames. In the end, you will have four frames screwed together with wing

screws so that you can easily assemble and disassemble the enclosure. Another frame with somewhat sturdier fine wire mesh serves as a cover. Fasten two hinges on one side and one or two latches on the opposite side so that you can easily open the cover like the lid of a trunk.

Weatherproof shelter: A sturdy shelter is absolutely necessary. If you intend to leave the animals in the outdoor enclosure only during the day, you can purchase a weatherproof hide box in the pet store. If the animals will be staying outdoors day and night, I urge you to get a house that will withstand wind, weather, and cold. I had a carpenter build a house for my guinea pigs, but here's a tip on how you can build one yourself: A shelter with a base measuring 16 × 16 inches (40 × 40 cm) and a height of 12 inches (30 cm) is large enough for two animals. The floor of the shelter is made of solid wood. So that the "guinea pig mansion" doesn't rest directly on the ground, you can nail or screw "feet" about 1 inch (2.5 cm) high to the underside of the floor. Then screw wood blocks about 2 inches (5 cm) high to the top of the base on all four sides; these will serve to anchor the house. The house fits over the wood blocks, which makes it easy to remove and clean. The walls and the roof are made of wood 3/4 to 1 inch (2 to 2.5 cm) thick, and the roof is slightly sloped so that water can run off. To protect the roof, apply a coat of nontoxic varnish or paint, which cannot harm the animals. The entrance should be 4 inches (10 cm) wide and 4-3/4 inches (12 cm) high. I use a board that is 1/3 inch (8 mm) thick as an entrance ramp, which allows the animals to run into the shelter easily if danger threatens. I cover the floor of the shelter with bedding, and in cold weather I add some straw.

The right location for the outdoor enclosure

Choose a place in the yard that is level and sheltered from the wind; it's best if it offers both sun and shade. A spot under a tree is ideal. If that's not possible, then lay a tarp (canvas) over the cover so

---

Beware of Intruders

UNWELCOME VISITORS: Skunks, raccoons, opossums, rats, foxes, and cats prey on guinea pigs.

SAFETY: Lay down stone slabs or fine wire mesh on the ground inside the enclosure and cover this with a thick layer of soil. The enclosure can be protected from above with wire mesh stretched over wooden frames.

---

that the animals get some shade. A shady site is absolutely essential for guinea pig survival, because they can quickly succumb to heatstroke. Guinea pigs are not able to regulate their body temperature as well as animals like dogs and cats. When setting up a movable outdoor enclosure, also remember that the position of the sun changes. If there is too much wind, it helps to fasten a sheet of plastic along one side of the enclosure.

Vacation on the balcony

You don't really need a yard to let your guinea pigs get a bit of fresh air. Your pets will also be happy on the balcony or patio if you keep a few things in mind.
> Balconies or patios must be sheltered from the wind. Provide a wind screen if necessary.
> The lower part of balcony railings must be covered with bricks, boards, or wire mesh so that the guinea pigs cannot fall or hurt themselves.
> Provide protection from the sun, as in the yard.
> An enclosure on the balcony or patio needs a weatherproof shelter.
> A net over the enclosure or a frame covered with wire mesh will protect your animals from birds of prey.
> A stone floor is either too cold or too warm and can easily lead to joint problems. Cover the floor with grass mats (page 23).
> Create a stimulating environment for the animals by furnishing the enclosure with interesting toys.

Gentle Acclimation for Sensitive Animals

Whether dog, cat, or guinea pig, making the transition to different surroundings and meeting strangers—either humans or others of their kind—is always hard on the animals and causes a great deal of stress. Everything is new, and the animals have to come to terms with that. A responsible pet owner should be aware of this at all times and treat the new family members with kindness and understanding.

In the first few days, guinea pigs don't make it easy for us to imagine what they're going through. They just sit there calmly in the cage, cool as a cucumber and apparently without a care in the world. But they are under a tremendous amount of strain. The heart is beating wildly and stress hormones are flooding the body. Guinea pigs are sensitive animals, and you have to keep that in mind. If you do, you will lay the foundation for a happy relationship and derive a great deal of pleasure from these cuddly little creatures.

At this point, I would like to reiterate how important it is to buy more than one animal. This is the young animals' first separation from the herd. That triggers anxiety and a feeling of abandonment. In a group, though, the guinea pigs support each other; as they say, a sorrow shared is a sorrow halved. The first days are important, and it all begins with the trip to their new home.

Traveling with care

Don't put an animal in a box all by itself; instead, buy a plastic travel carrier. It's a bit expensive, but the investment will pay off. You can also use the carrier for other purposes, like trips to the veterinarian or taking the animals out into the backyard enclosure. A travel carrier has major advantages: The animals can move around freely inside, and the air is much better than in a small box. Put some bedding from the "old" cage in the carrier.

It will alleviate the guinea pigs' anxiety and give them a feeling of security because it still smells like

An inquisitive newcomer inspects everything in these unfamiliar surroundings. The shadowy interior of a woven grass hut makes a marvelous hiding place.

their old cage. And where should the carrier go in the car? It's best to put it on a seat and secure it with a seat belt. The trunk is not a good place, because the air is bad there.

Moving into the new home

Home at last! Now what? Here are a few tips that have worked well for me:

Temptation: Slices of carrot scattered around the cage will tempt the animals to explore their new home from top to bottom. Don't disturb your pets at this time; instead, watch them carefully. Once they accept food and water, they've cleared the first hurdle on the way to acclimation.

Making acclimation easier: Avoid loud slamming of doors, shrill high-pitched sounds, and hectic activity. As long as the guinea pigs are still shy and skittish, they should not be handled or picked up. Don't turn the lights on and off too frequently. In the first weeks, clean only the especially dirty parts of the cage. The scent of their own cage gives

them a sense of security and makes the cage feel like home. This way you can help the guinea pigs settle in quickly.

How guinea pigs become tame

What is the quickest way to tame guinea pigs? That is one of the questions I'm most frequently asked to answer. I can certainly understand it, because tame guinea pigs are simply more enjoyable. My suggestion consists of four steps:

Win their trust: Don't force the animals to do anything. Let the guinea pigs come to you of their own free will. Speak to them softly and leave the cage door closed. Imitate guinea pig sounds. They can't resist "guinea pig language." It's best if you're at eye level with the animals. That way you don't look so huge, and the animals feel less threatened.

A gentle touch: Rub your hands with cage bedding and use a carrot to tempt your little band to come closer. Stick the carrot through the cage wires and say, "gooood." This way the animals get used to your voice and associate something positive with you. Touch the guinea pigs when you feed them. After several sessions, you may pet them.

Treats work wonders: From the guinea pig's viewpoint, you are associated with only positive, pleasant experiences. You can build upon this by tempting the guinea pig out of her cage with treats like a piece of carrot or a sprig of parsley. If she comes out of the cage without hesitation, scratch her gently under the chin.

The guinea pig has settled in and will leave her familiar cage even without "temptations."

Hello, partner: The ice has been broken. Now it's just a question of reinforcing the taming process. If you practice enticing your pets out of the cage and petting them two or three times a day, you'll soon be good friends. Before long the guinea pigs will want to be around you. They are always ready for a little cuddling, especially if they can expect a treat afterward as a reward.

1 GETTING ACQUAINTED: Give your new housemates time to become familiar with their surroundings and get to know you better. Sit down next to the cage, leaving the cage door closed for the time being. Speak quietly to the animals and imitate guinea pig sounds. Don't force the guinea pigs to do anything.

2 A LITTLE "TEMPTATION": The way to a guinea pig's heart is through her stomach. Rub your hands with a bit of cage bedding so that you don't smell like a stranger. Then extend a piece of carrot or a sprig of parsley through the closed cage door. Speak softly to your pet. After a few attempts, repeat the whole process with the door open.

3 YOU'VE WON THEIR TRUST: Now the animals know you and associate positive things with you. Open the cage door and build a path from the opened door to the floor of the room; you could use a flexible wooden bridge for this. Lure your guinea pigs out of the cage with a treat. If they hurry over eagerly, you have won their trust.

When Guinea Pigs Become Parents

Being around guinea pig babies is a fantastic experience. What happens during courtship and mating, how mother and babies (called pups) interact, how the little ones grow up . . . With a bit of luck, you might even witness a birth. No doubt about it, I wouldn't want to have missed these experiences, and they gave me a deeper understanding of guinea pig biology. Nevertheless, you have to curb your enthusiasm if you don't know what to do with the offspring. That is the most important rule, because it's not uncommon for the guinea pigs to wander from one owner to another before winding up in an animal shelter. This instability is terrible for the animals and triggers an enormous amount of stress. That's why you must give careful consideration to whether you really want to assume the additional work and responsibility.

Lots of offspring—a survival strategy

Domestic guinea pigs, like their wild cousins, have lots of offspring. In the wild, producing many young is part of their survival strategy, because guinea pigs have practically no weapons they can use to defend themselves against their enemies. They are easily captured by birds of prey and small predators. Having babies, and lots of them, is the key to their success. This reproductive strategy is the reason guinea pigs are among the most common rodents in South America.

Female guinea pigs are sexually mature at just three weeks of age, although they are not full grown until they are two months old. Unfortunately, very young females run a great risk of giving birth to malformed offspring if they are mated too soon. That's why you should separate these females temporarily from the males by housing them in their own cage.

The correct way to pick up a guinea pig: Place one hand around the animal's chest and immediately support the hindquarters with the other hand.

How to Keep Your Animals Happy

Here's the recipe for harmonious coexistence of humans and guinea pigs: learn to understand the animals, encourage their trust from the very first day, give them a large cage, and provide daily out-of-cage time with plenty of physical and mental stimulation.

This is good This is not

+ Right from the start, make contact with the animals by speaking to them quietly and "tempting" them with a treat.

+ The voice of their owner and the chattering of the other herd members calm guinea pigs.

+ Exploring new surroundings in the family group encourages curiosity. Grassy areas with rocks, pieces of wood, dens, and passageways are always a hit.

+ Spend time with your animals. For example, tempt them over an obstacle with a treat.

− Guinea pigs are active during the day but still take naps at certain times. Don't disturb the animals when they're resting.

− Avoid slamming doors, blaring music, shrill sounds, and raised voices near the animals.

− Guinea pigs should not be exposed to direct sun and bright light. Provide areas of shade indoors as well as in the outdoor enclosure.

− Don't force the guinea pigs to do anything. No punishment! Don't pick the animals up roughly.

Tip: Having babies takes a lot of energy, so make sure that the parents are healthy. A mother pregnant with three youngsters, which weigh about 2 to 3 ounces (60 to 80 g) at birth, is carrying about one-third of her body weight.

The guinea pig's courtship

Courtship appears to be anything but romantic. And forget about exchanging tokens of affection! The "suitor" gets right to the point. He sniffs at the female's nose, head, sides, back, and genital region, then nudges her flanks. He circles her in slow motion and displays his testicles briefly and repeatedly. In the process, he "purrs" audibly. If his wooing is successful, he mounts her. A female ready to mate shows her willingness by stretching her hind legs and lifting her rump. Copulation, from the human point of view, is very brief, lasting about 15 to 30 seconds. In the animal kingdom, times

Just after birth, guinea pig pups already look like miniature versions of their parents. The mother nurses them for only three weeks.

this short are not unusual. Even chimpanzees, our closest relatives, copulate very quickly. After mating, the guinea pigs lick their genitals. A minute or more later, they begin to mate again. To be certain that he really is the father of the offspring, the male seals the female's vagina with a copulatory plug, which falls out a few hours later. If the object of the male's affections is not in a receptive mood, she gives him a "urine shower." The spray is usually effective, and the suitor retreats. Females are able to conceive only for a few hours. If they do not mate, their next eggs ripen 16 days later, and the courtship ritual starts all over again.

Fit from an early age

Pregnancy in guinea pigs last an average of 68 days. Usually two to four young "pups" are born. It's rare for a mother to have just one baby. Guinea pig mothers-to-be seek out a quiet and protected place for themselves. Unlike most other rodents, though, they do not build a nest or dig a hole. Witnessing a birth is more or less a matter of chance, because the behavior of the pregnant female reveals very little about the time of birth.

My guinea pigs never had problems giving birth. Usually everything was over in half an hour. The behavior of the other herd members was remarkable: They kept perfectly still throughout the entire process. The newborns made soft, high-pitched sounds.

Birth: Labor begins about 20 minutes before delivery. When giving birth, the female crouches and bears down, her hind legs spread apart. The pup appears headfirst. Then the mother pulls the newborn out from beneath her belly between her hind and front legs and frees it from the fetal membranes.

There is an affectionate relationship between mother and baby. If the mother is too far away, the little one gets her attention by squealing; then the mother guinea pig hurries over to see what's bothering her youngster.

The babies have arrived: And what do the pups look like? Actually, they're like the adults, fully furred but smaller. They even lose their baby teeth while still in the mother's womb. No wonder the mother doesn't lavish care on them. She licks her offspring pups dry and nurses them for three weeks. From the very first day, the little ones eat solid food.

Although it's true that guinea pig mothers don't have as much work rearing their young as other

Giving the Pups Away

I think the best time to give away the young guinea pigs is two weeks after they stop nursing. While still pups, the guinea pigs learn the rules of the herd and discover their own role and position in the group. This is especially important for males.

animal mothers, their pregnancy is all the more strenuous. As mentioned, the babies are almost fully developed at birth; that is unbelievably taxing and requires a lot of energy. For this reason, you should feed a pregnant female more fresh foods and pellets and be sure to give her 20 mg of vitamin C a day. That is approximately twice the dose the animals normally need. Females must have a rest between litters. Hence my tip: Your guinea pig should not have pups more than once or at most twice a year.

Tip: Surprisingly, the mother comes into heat again shortly after birth. For this reason, you should separate the father and mother no later than one hour after the pups are born. To be on the safe side, separate the pair two days before the suspected delivery date.

Development of the young

Immediately after birth, the pups are so independent that they move around on their short little legs, exploring the world with open eyes. Guinea pig pups are typical "precocial" animals, which means they are well developed and able to care for themselves at birth. Hygiene is already part of their daily routine. They groom themselves frequently and are quite adept at it. Nothing can keep them from suckling from their mother's nipples occasionally, though. The mother has two nipples in the groin area. But what happens if there are four pups and only two nipples? Quite simple: If other nursing mothers are around, the pups go to their "aunt" and help themselves. If the mother is alone, though, the pups must wait their turn, although that's really not a problem for guinea pigs. After about 21 to 30 days, mama's "milk bar" finally closes.

The littermates stay close to each other. They keep track of each other using "contact calls." Animals of the same age band together in groups. They sleep and rest close together, too. The mother watches over her pups attentively. As soon as a youngster squeals, she comes running over.

And what do the youngsters do? They play and investigate everything. One game, called "popcorning," is especially comical and always fun to watch. Without warning, they suddenly jump into the air from a standing position.

Guinea pigs grow up quickly. From birth to adulthood takes only a few weeks. Males are sexually mature between six to ten weeks of age and are already able to breed at two and a half months. Females ovulate for the first time at just four weeks of age and should be mated before they are 12 months old.

Raising Orphaned Animals

NEWBORNS: They eat on their own shortly after birth but need a replacement for mother's milk.

MILK REPLACER: This formula has worked well. You can find the recipe on the back flap under the heading "Nutritional Deficiency."

CHOKING: Feed slowly so that the pups don't choke.

MATING: In guinea pigs, the process is not especially romantic or spectacular. The male sniffs the female, nudges her flanks with his nose, and circles her in slow motion, all the while repeatedly displaying his testicles and "purring" at her. If the female is ready to mate, she straightens her hind legs and raises her rump. Copulation itself lasts only 15 to 30 seconds in guinea pigs.

THREE DAYS OLD: Although young guinea pigs are nursed by their mother for the first three weeks, they eat solid food on their own from the day they're born. Even shortly after birth, the little ones spend a lot of time playing. A favorite game is leaping straight up into the air ("popcorning"). This is how they train their muscles and develop agility. It's comical to watch these little bundles of fur behaving this way.

MOTHER AND BABY: This guinea pig is only three weeks old and is no longer nursing. Nevertheless, the mother still keeps a watchful eye on her offspring.

Guaranteed Happy and Healthy

A proper diet and regular care are the most important requirements for keeping your pets healthy. Guinea pigs can still
get sick, though. If this happens, don't hesitate to consult a
veterinarian right away. The earlier the problem is diagnosed,
the better the chances of a complete recovery.

A Healthy Diet: What Guinea Pigs Need

"You are what you eat." This old saying still holds true and is more important today than ever. It applies to both humans and animals. The health of any creature depends on what it eats. In animals, a poor diet is often reflected in the coat or teeth. But what actually constitutes a good diet?

What's healthy for one species can harm another. Why, for instance, does even a moderate amount of chocolate harm guinea pigs, but not us? The answer lies in the past, in the history of the species.

Over the millennia, each species has adapted to its food. Guinea pigs are plant eaters (herbivores), lions are meat eaters (carnivores), and we humans eat everything and anything (omnivores). Compared with carnivores, herbivores have a long intestine. The intestine of a guinea pig is more than 8 feet (2.5 m) long. To get an idea of how incredibly long this is, compare it with the intestine of a much larger human, which measures only 20 feet (6 m) in length.

Strict vegetarians

Herbivores spend almost the entire day eating, although the portions they consume are always relatively small. That makes them fundamentally different from carnivores. Lions can eat 40 pounds (18 kg) of meat at a time. That's why you should feed your guinea pigs small amounts several times a day. The intestine of the little rodents practically cries out for foods high in crude fiber. Without a steady supply of food, movement of the intestine (peristalsis) slows down, because the intestinal musculature is weakly developed. Consequently, guinea pigs should not go hungry.

Whether human, lion, or guinea pig, we all need specific amounts of carbohydrates, fat, and protein.

On the one hand, these substances supply energy; on the other, they are important for the renewal of our bodies. Guinea pigs are strict vegetarians. They can tolerate only plant protein. You wouldn't be doing your animals any favors if you gave them yogurt, cottage cheese, or perhaps meatballs.

Especially important

Above all, guinea pigs need hay. The hay rack should be kept full at all times. Because of its high fiber content, hay helps maintain intestinal motility, and, almost as a side effect, the constant chewing prevents teeth from overgrowing. I usually buy meadow hay so that I can give my animals a variety of plants. Check the package label to make sure the mixture contains plenty of herbs and that the hay is not too old. Old hay is very dusty, has little nutri-

tional value, and smells musty. I buy hay in the pet store and have been quite happy with it. If you would like to enrich the hay, you can buy various dried herbs and mix them in.

Tip: Naturally, you can also collect edible plants yourself. But be careful! Don't collect plants along the sides of heavily traveled roads. The toxic exhaust contaminates the plants and will be bad for your guinea pigs' health as well. Plants from over-fertilized fields are also unhealthy. Suitable collecting sites include uncultivated and overgrown plots of land, fallow fields, old cemeteries, railroad embankments, and unspoiled meadows in nature preserves. Make sure that the plants you collect are not poisonous for your guinea pigs (text, left). You can find a wealth of information about poisonous plants on the Internet (Addresses, page 62).

A variety of greens

As important as hay is for guinea pigs, it cannot satisfy their energy requirements. It's easy to understand why. Hay consists of dried grasses and other herbaceous plants. During the drying process, many nutrients break down, and the hay no longer contains sufficient amounts of protein, fats, carbohydrates, vitamins, and minerals.

Fresh and juicy: Greens are essential for your guinea pigs' healthy diet because they contain plant proteins, carbohydrates, oils, vitamins, and trace elements. Keep in mind, though, that the nutrient content of young plants is higher than that of older plants. Moreover, too much of a good thing can be dangerous. This is particularly true in the spring. Spring grass contains a great deal of protein and very little crude fiber, and this can lead to digestive upsets. Introduce your animals slowly to fresh grass and herbs. You have to be especially

Poisonous Plants

It is difficult to judge if a particular plant is poisonous. That's why I recommend that you feed only plants you know to be edible. You should not give your animals the following plants:

GARDEN PLANTS: acacia, angel's trumpet, autumn crocus, azalea, cherry laurel, columbine, crocus, ivy, jimsonweed, juniper, laburnum, mercury, monkshood, nightshades, periwinkle, pheasant's-eye, Solomon's seal, spurges, wisteria, yew, and any members of the buttercup and lily families.

HOUSEPLANTS: Benjamin fig, crown of thorns, cyclamen, dieffenbachia, ferns, hoya, Jerusalem cherry, oleander, and poinsettia.

A pot planted with various herbs or grass seeds provides fresh food indoors or during the winter.

No easy task! It takes persistence and agility to reach the tasty morsels, but that keeps the animals from becoming bored.

careful with vitamins, because guinea pigs, just like us humans, cannot manufacture their own vitamin C. They can get it only from their food. That's why I recommend that you add a pinch of vitamin C powder (from the drugstore or pharmacy) to the food, just to be on the safe side. This is especially true in the winter months when fresh greens are harder to find.

Tasty!: The greens on my guinea pigs' menu vary with the season. I try to buy vegetables at the market and wash them carefully with lukewarm water. My animals like to eat dandelion greens (not too much, though, because they contain a lot of calcium and protein), carrots, cucumbers, broccoli, cauliflower leaves, spinach, zucchini, celery, chickweed, field mint, coltsfoot, calendula, and chamomile. They also enjoy chicory, head lettuce, and iceberg lettuce. My guinea pigs are not particularly fond of fruit. I keep offering it, but without much success. Now and then they eat a piece of apple or pear.

To meet their mineral requirement, I offer my guinea pigs a salt lick.

Tip: Feed chicory sparingly. Be careful with cabbage and clover. Too much can cause intestinal gas.

Pros and cons of commercial guinea pig diets

Opinions differ on commercial guinea pig diets. Opponents maintain that they make animals gain too much weight and that even homemade food is healthier. I have had satisfactory results with commercial diets. The important thing is not to feed too much. Give no more than one to two tablespoons of pellet mix per animal per day. These mixtures usually contain wheat, oats, corn, sunflower seeds, peanuts, and small pellets of compressed hay supplemented with vitamins and minerals. Don't buy too much at once, because pellet mixes spoil quickly. Although commercial foods are called "nutritionally complete diets," this term

Chubby Guinea Pigs

CAUSES	Obesity in guinea pigs can be caused by many factors, including too much food, unhealthy treats, too little exercise, and stress. Even genetics plays a role. If guinea pigs are exposed to unfamiliar partners every day, the resulting anxiety can make them gain weight. Thus, social conditions are also an important factor.
WHAT TO DO?	If your guinea pig is overweight, then give him a little less food. Conscientiously avoid high-calorie foods like treat sticks. Try to whet your little butterball's curiosity so that he gets more exercise and slims down naturally (page 50 and following).
NEVER	Guinea pigs should never be allowed to go hungry. They must always have small portions of food available throughout the day.

is somewhat misleading because it implies that the animals need no other food. However, that's not the case. Your guinea pigs need hay and greens every day.

Something to chew on

Rodents' teeth grow throughout their lives. Overgrown teeth interfere with eating and cause injuries. That's why chewable items are a must: They keep the teeth from growing too long. I let my guinea pigs chew on hard bread and unsprayed twigs from apple, pear, linden, and birch trees. Now and then you can even spoil your animals with a chew treat or chew stick from the pet store. Be careful with snacks like these, though. Although it's true that guinea pigs love them, they contain a lot of sugar. Such high-calorie treats will make the animals gain too much weight if given too often.

Water is the best drink

Even with juicy greens in their diet, guinea pigs need about 3 ounces (100 ml) of fresh water a day. In hot weather, the animals drink big gulps from their water bottle. Water must be readily available at all times.

Make sure that you clean the metal tube of the sipper bottle thoroughly every day so that germs can't lodge there (page 43).

Guinea Pig Care Made Easy

Pets are dependent on our care to help them stay clean and healthy. In nature, the animals can solve the problem themselves, and they do a good job of it. Have you ever seen a filthy animal in the wild? For animals, a mud bath isn't dirt, it's a substitute for soap. Proper care is just as important as healthy food. Caring for your guinea pigs includes cleaning their living areas as well as grooming them. Regular cleaning of the cage, pen, and accessories is a basic requirement for keeping your guinea pigs healthy. Otherwise, viruses, bacteria, and fungi would have an easy time of it, and your guinea pigs would fall victim to disease in no time.

Cleaning the cage and accessories

My housekeeping schedule for my guinea pigs looks like this:

Every day I wash the food bowls and water bottles with hot water. It's best to clean the sipper bottle with a bottle brush and the metal tube with a cotton swab. In less than ten minutes, the job is finished and the guinea pigs are eating and drinking from clean dishes.

Once a week, a major cleanup is in order. I replace the bedding and clean the entire cage, including the furnishings. Meanwhile, I put the animals in the indoor exercise area or in the outdoor pen, depending on the weather. My cleaning tools are a brush and hot water. I don't use detergents or chemical cleaning products. Toys, bricks, and partitions are washed with hot water and scrubbed with the brush. I tackle heavily soiled areas with dilute citric acid or vinegar. I put the plastic tray and wire cage top in the bath tub or under the shower and rinse off both with hot water.

Grooming guinea pigs

With guinea pigs, the type of grooming depends on the breed. Long-haired animals need a lot of care, whereas smooth-coated ones need very little. However, they all require a certain minimum. Before you begin, you should know how to pick up and carry your pets properly. With most animals this is not a problem, but you have to be careful with guinea pigs. When you pick up an animal, clasp his chest from below with one hand and support his hindquarters with your other hand (photo, page 32). Carry the guinea pig by placing him on your flexed lower arm, which should be

Long-haired Silkie guinea pigs have to be combed and brushed several times a week so that their coats don't become matted.

held close to your upper body so that he can't slip through. With your other hand prevent the animal from falling.

Coat care: Smooth-coated guinea pigs need to be combed and brushed only when they are very dirty. As a rule they usually keep their coats clean by themselves. With long-haired guinea pigs it's a different story. Their long hair is too much for them to handle, and they should be combed with a coarse comb and brushed with a soft brush several times a week. In the wild, animals like this would have very little chance of surviving. To comb and brush an animal, place him on a warmed towel either on the table or on your lap. Guinea pigs really enjoy this. Run your hand over the entire coat, starting at the rump. This way you will feel any skin lesions or matted areas in the coat. Heavily matted hair must be sheared professionally by a veterinarian. Don't let it get this far, though. Give your long-haired animals a short haircut, especially in summer.

Toenails: Be sure to pay attention to the length of the toenails, because overgrown nails cause the animal pain. A hard floor usually keeps

Guinea pigs love woven grass hideaways. They can nibble on them without risk, run in and out of them, or use them as a safe lookout from which to watch what's going on outside.

the nails worn down; at least it takes longer until they have to be trimmed again. The first time you cut the toenails, it's best to have a veterinarian show you the proper technique.

Teeth: Incisors grow throughout the animal's life. What's an advantage in the wild can become a handicap in domestic animals. If the animals don't get enough hard foods, the teeth may curve inward as they grow, making it difficult for the animals to eat. That's why it is essential that you check the teeth regularly and provide plenty of items for chewing (photo, page 41). Overgrown teeth have to be trimmed by the veterinarian.

Eyes, ears, nose: Use a warm, damp cloth to carefully wipe away any accumulated discharge or dirt from the eyes, ears, or nose. Caution: If the condition persists, you must take the animal to the veterinarian.

Weight monitoring: A guinea pig's weight is an important indicator of his state of health. That's why you should weigh your animals regularly (photo, page 48).

Like most animals, including humans, overweight animals develop health problems as time goes by (page 42). That's not unusual. However, if an animal loses up to 10 percent of his weight over the space of a few days, you have to take action. Clearly something is wrong in the group, the guinea pig is under too much stress, or he is sick. Consult a veterinarian.

Grooming and Housekeeping Schedule

GOOD HYGIENE PREVENTS DISEASE

DAILY	Rinse out water bottles and food bowls with hot water. Don't use dish detergent! Check teeth, anus, eyes, nose, and ears. Short-haired guinea pigs groom themselves but love being massaged with a soft natural-bristle brush. Long-haired guinea pigs should be combed and brushed daily.
WEEKLY	Clean cage and accessories under hot water, and then dry them thoroughly. Replace all bedding. Scrub water bottles (sipper bottles) with a bottle brush and clean the metal sipper tube thoroughly with a cotton swab. Replace the bedding in the "rooting box" (pages 50 and 57).
MONTHLY	If bladder sludge has accumulated in the bottom tray, it can be dissolved with dilute citric acid (from the pharmacy) or softened in vinegar. Then rinse out the bottom tray with hot water and dry it well.
AS NECESSARY	After an illness, it is a good idea to disinfect the cage and accessories with a mild disinfectant. Consult your veterinarian.

When the Guinea Pig Gets Sick

Good husbandry and proper care prevent disease. Besides, our guinea pigs are robust creatures. In all the years I have been keeping guinea pigs, I have rarely had to take them to a veterinarian. My dogs and even my parakeets got sick more often. However, if you notice that one of your animals is unusually apathetic or behaving abnormally, then don't delay. Take your pet to the veterinarian. Guinea pigs have a high metabolic rate. A few figures will illustrate this. The heart, which weighs 1/16 ounce (2.1 g), beats 230 to 380 times a minute. That is much faster than ours (50 to 80 heartbeats per minute on average). Their body temperature is between 100 and 103.5°F (37.9 and 39.7°C). This high metabolic rate is also responsible for the fact that germs spread quickly in their body,

Liquid medicines are best squirted into the side of the mouth using a pipette. Have the veterinarian demonstrate this technique for you.

so that even small infections can become life-threatening. That's why, for humans as well as guinea pigs, an ounce of prevention is worth a pound of cure.

› Physical activity is important because guinea pigs have a tendency to put on weight. Make sure they get plenty of exercise.

› Put your animals in the outdoor enclosure whenever possible. Fresh air strengthens their resistance and is good for their coat, skin, and lungs.

› Solitary guinea pigs are much more susceptible to stress and disease. Loneliness makes them sick.

› Pay attention to the composition of the group. Harmony in the herd determines the health and well-being of its members.

› Beware of cold, damp stone floors, especially balcony tiles.

› Hygiene is important. Leftover food and feces are an ideal breeding ground for germs.

› The bedding must be dry, never soaking wet.

Recognizing signs of disease

How can you tell if guinea pigs are sick or are coming down with something? Naturally, in a small manual like this one, I can only touch on the most common disease symptoms; your veterinarian has to make a precise diagnosis. The following signs indicate that a guinea pig needs help:

› The animal eats and drinks much less than usual.

› The animal loses about 10 percent of his total weight within a three-day period.

› The guinea pig sits apathetically in the cage.

› The animal has an elevated temperature. The normal temperature is 100 to 103.5°F (37.9 to

Common Diseases of Guinea Pigs

SYMPTOMS	CAUSES	TREATMENT
Anal region and hind legs are stained and caked with feces; hindquarters are conspicuously raised.	DIARRHEA: caused by spoiled food, contaminated drinking water, or a change in diet.	Give hay and slightly sweetened chamomile tea; see a veterinarian if symptoms persist more than two days.
Severe itching with scratching and biting; circular areas of hair loss.	FUNGAL INFECTION: These are almost always very stubborn diseases	Diagnosis and treatment by a veterinarian, who will culture the fungus.
Severe itching; epilepsy-like convulsions; flaky skin; thickened skin on head, neck, and shoulders; bleeding and crusty wounds caused by scratching.	INFESTATION WITH MANGE MITES (SARCOPTID MITES): The itching results from an allergic reaction to the mites parasitizing the skin. Disease triggers: stress, poor husbandry, improper diet.	Definitely consult the veterinarian, because a severe mite infestation can lead to the animal's death. Improve the husbandry conditions.
Various swellings around the head, neck, shoulders, and back; 3/4 to 2 inches (2 to 5 cm) in diameter; skin covering them is often hairless; rarely painful.	ABSCESS, TUMOR, SEBACEOUS GLAND ADENOMA: These are possible causes.	Diagnosis and treatment by a veterinarian. It is usually suggested that these be removed surgically under anesthesia.
The animal eats less, despite having a good appetite; drooling; hair around the mouth is caked with saliva.	MISALIGNED TEETH (MALOCCLUSION): Predominantly affects the lower cheek teeth, which grow from both sides and can actually form a bridge over the tongue.	Diagnosis and treatment by a veterinarian.
Inflamed swellings on the pads of the feet, which can also bleed and fester.	FOOTPAD INFECTIONS (PODODERMATITIS): These usually prove to be extremely stubborn and chronic.	Diagnosis and treatment by a veterinarian with antibiotics, surgery, ointment dressings.
Fatigue, trembling, paralysis of the hindquarters, shortness of breath.	GUINEA PIG PARALYSIS, BACTERIAL RESPIRATORY INFECTION, FOOD POISONING, VIRAL PNEUMONIA: Various causes are possible.	Diagnosis and treatment by a veterinarian.
Apathy, lying on one side and panting, bluish mucous membranes.	HEATSTROKE: Guinea pigs cannot tolerate direct sunlight.	Immediately get the animal into the shade. Place his feet in a shallow dish of water.

39.7°C). Use a digital thermometer to take the animal's temperature, because it is easier to read. Smear the tip of the thermometer with a little petroleum jelly and insert it carefully into the anus.

Tip: Never treat a sick animal with medications from your own medicine cabinet. That can be dangerous for the little creature. Although it's true that most drugs have been developed and tested in animals, you rarely know which species were used as experimental animals. An infrared lamp is useful as first aid and for mild colds. It stimulates metabolism and circulation. The lamp should illuminate only one side of the cage, though, so that the animal can freely choose to leave the heated area. To avoid the danger of infection, I separate the patient from the other members of the herd and put him in a travel carrier or another cage. If possible, arrange it so he can hear the other guinea pigs.

The guinea pig patient

Traveling to the veterinarian: It's best to put the animal in a travel carrier (from the pet store) for the trip to the veterinarian. A handful of bedding from his cage makes the guinea pig feel secure. If you carry the animal in your arms, he will panic quickly.

Liquid medications: The best way to administer drops prescribed by the veterinarian is to squirt them into the side of the mouth behind the incisors using a pipette (photo, page 46). Keep a firm hold on the guinea pig with your other hand.

Ointments: Use a cotton swab to apply ointments. Find out from the veterinarian precisely how much of the medication to use and where to apply it. Never just put some ointment on your finger and then rub it on the animal; you'll run the risk of infection!

Parasites

Like all animals, guinea pigs can become infested by parasites. These pests can cause severe skin diseases. Candidates that can attack guinea pigs are mites, fleas, biting lice, and even fungi. These are called "ectoparasites." Infestation can often be attributed to poor husbandry and improper diet. The average pet owner knows little

A change in weight can be a sign of illness. That's why you should weigh your guinea pigs regularly.

about the different risks posed by fleas, mites, biting lice, and fungi. That's why a diagnosis by the veterinarian is absolutely necessary. Fleas and lice are not terribly dangerous, but they still have to be controlled. Mites, on the other hand, are nasty customers for guinea pigs. A heavy infestation of mites can lead to the death of an animal. Mites are arachnids, and some, like mange mites (*Trixacarus caviae*), can burrow into the skin. The itching makes the guinea pig scratch. This leads to flaking skin and scratch wounds. Experts believe a weakened immune system may be an underlying factor in severe mite infestations. The veterinarian usually administers an injection to control these parasites and for chronic infections prescribes a special shampoo to bathe the animal.

The medicinal bath

Bathing a guinea pig is advisable only when prescribed by the veterinarian. To give a medicinal bath, I put the animal in a bucket of lukewarm water. The guinea pig stands on his hind legs while I support him by grasping him below the front paws with my left hand; the animal's head remains above the water. I rub his head gently with the shampoo solution, being careful not to get any soap in the little patient's eyes. After the bath, dry the guinea pig off thoroughly and be sure to keep him out of drafts or he will catch cold.

Important Information about Disease

TIPS FROM
GUINEA PIG EXPERT
Immanuel Birmelin

REST: A sick guinea pig needs lots of rest and close observation. Look in on your patient several times a day and check his breathing and activity.

RISK OF COLDS: Guinea pigs catch cold easily, so bathe your animals only if they are infested with parasites or if the veterinarian has prescribed it. On the other hand, they enjoy a brief rain shower in their outdoor enclosure. It rids the coat of dust and dirt and massages the skin. Guinea pigs know what's good for them, and if they get too wet, they'll run for shelter.

CECOTROPES: Guinea pigs eat their feces. Although you might think this is disgusting, it is essential for your pets. These are not normal feces, though, but soft, moist droppings called "cecotropes." By eating them, guinea pigs obtain needed protein.

DEATH: An animal suffering from an incurable or very painful disease should be put to sleep (euthanized) by the veterinarian.

Activity Keeps Them Fit

Guinea pigs are truly "active" when they have something new to explore. Both body and mind have to be challenged; otherwise they get rusty. It's really not hard to make sure our lovable little pets have lots of variety and excitement in their life. Simply put the following suggestions into action.

Guinea Pigs Love Variety

Guinea pigs have a bad reputation. In contrast to rats, they are considered to be a bit stupid and not especially teachable. However, if you get involved with the little critters and remove their fears, you'll be surprised at how quick they are to learn.

Overcoming fear

Guinea pigs are flight animals, which is why caution plays such an important role in their life. If you want to teach guinea pigs something, you must help them overcome this cautiousness or fear. If, on the other hand, the animals feel safe and secure, they're eager to go exploring. They sniff at everything they encounter and test every object with their incisors; from an elevated perch, they survey their surroundings with interest. Guinea pigs are anything but stupid. For example, my animals learned how to find their way out of a complicated maze in no time. What many believed to be almost impossible, my guinea pigs accomplished with élan. They unerringly pressed the correct colored keys to receive a food reward and thus demonstrated that they can recognize colors. As already mentioned, this presupposes that the animals are happy and unafraid. If you follow these rules, you can teach your guinea pigs a few little tricks. Morsels of food (carrots or cucumbers) really work wonders as a motivational aid. Your guinea pigs will learn what's expected of them in a flash. Their memory is amazing, too. A year after we carried out the experiments in which the animals had to press keys, we repeated the tests and found that they had no trouble with them whatsoever. They pressed the keys just as accurately and as quickly as they did on the final day the year before.

They even remembered complicated tasks a year later. No doubt about it, guinea pigs are often underestimated. No one could imagine that guinea pigs would get bored and become apathetic when frustrated by lack of activity. Nevertheless, boredom is a serious problem for almost all animals under human care, be they zoo animals or pets. In the wild, animals must forage for food, defend themselves from predators, and deal with rivals. Pets are spared all of that, though. Activities become a substitute for the living conditions and tasks that guinea pigs face in the wild. Providing activities for your guinea pigs is a must if you want to give your animals the conditions they need as well as keep them mentally and physically fit.

How guinea pigs learn

Guinea pigs learn especially well at nine to ten months of age. That's relatively late when compared with dogs and cats. If you want to teach the little creatures something, in this case it's best to do it one at a time. Other guinea pigs will distract your pupil too much.

Recognizing voices: Guinea pigs quickly learn to distinguish voices. How can you test that? You need four people for this experiment, one standing at each corner of the cage. One person is well known to the guinea pig, and the other three are strangers. The familiar person calls the guinea pig with the same tone of voice used at feeding time. It doesn't usually take long for the animal to come running up. The guinea pig barely reacts to the other people. You can also teach a guinea pig to run to the place where she hears a low-pitched sound. How do you do that? When the guinea pig runs to the source of the low note, she gets a little piece of carrot. When she hears a high-pitched sound, she gets nothing. Repeat this process five to ten times, and the guinea pig will know what to do.

Testing sense of direction: In the wild guinea pigs must be able to find their way around. You can make use of this ability at home. Build a Y-shaped system of passageways using bricks, boards, or old books. The difference between the two passages is that the walls of one are covered with light-colored paper and the walls of the other are covered with dark paper. The animal's task is to get the food,

The ball is filled with hay or fresh foods and hung from the roof of the cage. A guinea pig has to be fit to get at the food.

which is located only in the light-colored passage. After four or five attempts, the animal will have learned where the food is. To be certain that the guinea pig is actually heading for the light side and not just going to the right or left, switch the light and dark sides.

How guinea pigs play

When young animals play, they are learning for later life. Especially during play, fitness and coordination can be developed without risk or pressure. Later on they can use the experience that they acquired as youngsters. That is essentially why animals play. Guinea pigs are not the most playful creatures in the animal kingdom; nevertheless, they do play, and young guinea pigs play tirelessly. They practice games of agility, leap into the air,

make twisty hops, and perform all sorts of antics. Games of tag are also part of their repertoire. Alternating between the hunter and the hunted, they chase each other to the point of exhaustion and then snuggle close together to rest. What's remarkable is that castrated animals enjoy playing even in old age. This is perfectly understandable, because they have the most "leisure time." They don't have to worry about choosing a mate or rearing young.

In one respect, though, guinea pigs are distinctly different from other herd animals. They don't engage in play-fighting of any kind. In many animal species, youngsters learn the rules of the group through mock battles. Evidently, the group behavior of guinea pigs is based on a different plan of study.

1 OBSTACLE COURSE: You can easily build this little obstacle course. Simply make a few poles from sections of branch and screw them onto a board.

2 TUNNEL SYSTEM: Drainage pipes can be turned into interesting objects for little "spelunkers." Perhaps they'll even find a "treasure" in the form of a treat.

3 SEESAW: A seesaw like this is another easy do-it-yourself project. This way your little rodents can develop their sense of balance.

Designs for Exciting Indoor and Outdoor Exercise Areas

Pet guinea pigs have a tendency to put on weight. That is understandable, because the South Americans Indians have been breeding them for meat for centuries. For them, guinea pigs are a source of food, like pigs are for us. This natural corpulence often causes problems. Excess weight presses on the legs and joints and puts a strain on the cardiovascular system. Obese animals are often short of breath and their life expectancy is reduced. A stimulating exercise area where the guinea pigs

can work off their surplus grams contributes to their well-being. That's why, even if the animals have a large cage, they should get several hours a day of free-roaming time either indoors or in their outdoor enclosure (page 23). At temperatures below 50°F (10°C), I recommend that you keep the animals indoors unless they are used to living outside. You can make the daily tour of the house exciting. Lay down scent trails, set up partitions, and much more . . . .

Recognizing shapes: You could draw a rectangle on one bowl and a circle on the other. Only one bowl, here the one with the circle, holds a reward.

Variety prevents boredom

Guinea pigs are the poster animals for scientific research. No wonder they have been used to demonstrate the effects of variety, in other words an exciting living area, on the rodent brain. The guinea pig's brain consists of millions of nerve cells. These are, to put it simply, the hardware. The type and frequency of connections between nerve cells (synapses) represent the software. Scientists studying guinea pigs realized that the more varied the environment, the more synapses they found. These neural connections could, however, be modified by learning or by providing an enriched environment. Like a construction site where scaffolding is constantly being erected, new connections are made and old ones are broken down. Science speaks clearly here, and every responsible zoo director knows that the animals' compounds must be designed to be interesting. Unfortunately, many pet owners still haven't heard this message.

Scientists at the University of Bern (Switzerland) are studying the effects of movable partitions on the behavior of the animals. If partitions are set up in the outdoor pen or indoor exercise area, the guinea pigs become more inquisitive and move around more. The animals enjoy jumping over them, provided they aren't too high; they can clear 4 inches (10 cm) with no trouble. The advantage of the partitions is that they are simple to set up and can easily be rearranged. You need one or two boards and four bricks, or something similar. Clamp each board between two bricks. It doesn't take much effort, but it has quite an effect.

Hazards Outside the Cage

HOW TO PROTECT YOUR GUINEA PIGS

INJURIES	Remove all sharp, pointed objects like needles, knives, thumbtacks, and spiny plants.
POISONING	Keep poisonous houseplants out of reach of the animals. Chemicals and cleaning products should also be inaccessible.
DOORS	Make sure that an animal doesn't get caught when you open or close doors.
TRAMPLING	Be careful where you walk when the animals are roaming around indoors. It's not uncommon for an owner to step on a guinea pig by accident and severely injure the animal.
ELECTROCUTION	Electrical wires must be kept out of reach of guinea pigs.
FALLS	Don't put the animal on a table. Cover the balcony and the porch with wire mesh or cat netting.
HEATSTROKE	Guinea pigs are susceptible to heatstroke. Make sure you provide areas of shade.
CATCHING COLD	Rugs and blankets prevent guinea pigs from catching cold on cold stone floors.

Fitness Trail for Guinea Pigs

Here are a few suggestions for turning your guinea pigs' indoor exercise area or outdoor pen into a playground:

Maze: Build a maze—using cardboard tubes, for instance—and place a piece of carrot at one end. Time how long it takes for an animal to navigate the maze and compare times for the first ten trials. You'll see how quickly your guinea pigs learn. Now rearrange the maze and record the times again. You can keep this game going for as long as you and the guinea pigs are having fun. In the outdoor enclosure, you can also create a maze using weatherproof drainage pipes from a home improvement center. The guinea pigs really enjoy romping around here (photo, page 53).

Seesaw: A seesaw helps your guinea pigs develop their sense of balance. It is important that the seesaw drop downward slowly when the animals run across it. A treat stimulates their curiosity (photo, page 53). You need a tree trunk about 6 inches (15 cm) long and about 4-3/4 inches (12 cm) in diameter; a board about 3/4 inch (2 cm) thick, 5-1/2 inches (13 cm) wide, and about 26 inches (65 cm) long; and some small branches. Attach the branches to the upper side of the board; this gives the animals better footing and keeps them from slipping.

Tubes in any shape—like these hollow logs—are always a hit with guinea pigs.

This wooden toy is safe to chew and can be used for "gymnastics."

Lookout tower: Make stairs by stacking several blocks of autoclaved aerated concrete ("air-crete") of various sizes or bricks of one size in a staggered pattern. You can buy the blocks at a home improvement center. Smooth any sharp edges with a wood file and apply a coat of nontoxic paint. Make sure that the stairs are stable.

Obstacle course: This develops not only the muscles, but agility as well. A course like this can be built in no time. All you need is a board for the base measuring 28 inches (71 cm) long by 5-1/2 inches (13 cm) wide, four sawn branches about 1-1/2 inches (4 cm) in diameter and 9-1/2 inches (24 cm) long, wood screws, and a screw driver. Simply attach the branches to the base using the screws (photo, page 53).

Woven grass hideaways: You can buy these in pet stores. Two or three hideaways marked with different scents make it more interesting for your guinea pigs. For example, you could rub one hideaway with fresh grass and the other with an animal's scent. Let your imagination run wild (photo, page 44).

Chew tree: This is very popular with my guinea pigs. I got the idea from well-known animal photographer Monika Wegler. The point of this chew tree is that the animals have to work for their food instead of just getting it put down in front of them. This idea is widely used nowadays as a way to provide activity for animals in zoos, and it has proven very successful. The chew tree consists of a forked branch or a square post with holes drilled in it. The branch or post is screwed onto a sturdy wooden base. Now fill the holes with a variety of treats, like carrots, parsley, and dandelion greens.

Cardboard box: Cut several doorways in a large shoe box (with lid)—an inexpensive way to entertain your guinea pigs.

There are such wonderful fresh scents outdoors! These beautiful dandelion blossoms are a real tasty treat for guinea pigs.

Rooting box: The little critters love to root around in a box filled with rustling straw or dry leaves. Cut a low entrance hole in the box so that the guinea pigs can climb in and out easily (photo, page 50).

Searching for food: Scatter treats like pieces of carrot or cucumber at different places in the outdoor enclosure, indoor pen, or during free-roaming time in the house. That will get your guinea pigs moving, and they will be rewarded with healthy treats. You can place a tasty morsel up high, for instance on a wooden bridge, so that the animal has to walk across the bridge to get it.

Care during vacation

Who doesn't look forward to vacation? You might not enjoy yourself as much, though, if you're worried about whether your animals are being well cared for. You shouldn't take your guinea pigs along with you on a trip. Unfamiliar surroundings and strange noises and smells frighten the animals. And here's another important tip: Don't separate the group, and don't put your animals in with an unfamiliar group of guinea pigs, such as a friend's herd. You wouldn't be doing yourself or your guinea pigs any favors, because the members of a herd are used to each other and every animal knows its social role. Separation can destroy the entire structure of the herd, and after vacation your animals will no longer get along. They will fight and tear into each other. Males are especially at risk.

What should you do, then, if you want to go on vacation? My personal choice is a pet sitter, someone I can rely on to care for my animals every day and give them lots of attention. Friends and acquaintances are best, of course, but sometimes it seems you're out of luck and nobody has time.

When you go on vacation, you should find a reliable pet sitter beforehand, because the animals don't like moving to different surroundings.

I have had good experiences with college students and older schoolchildren who want to earn a little extra money. First, though, you have to show the pet sitter exactly what needs to be done. Take the sitter along with you as you go through your daily round of pet care chores and explain everything. It's best if the sitter takes a few notes on how to carry out the assigned tasks. You and the sitter should take care of the animals together four or five times. This way the duties become routine and the sitter will get to know the animals.

If you absolutely cannot find a pet sitter, some pet stores or animal shelters will board your pets.

When guinea pigs grow old

Like all creatures, guinea pigs cannot avoid growing old. But the aging process of animals and humans differs considerably: In animals, it is usually shorter.

The majority of animals are capable of reproducing well into old age. Once they lose the ability to reproduce most of them die. Beloved grandmas and grandpas who help raise the young are a rarity. How long can guinea pigs live, then? The figures reported in the literature vary, with the life span said to be anywhere from 5 to 15 years. How long an organism survives certainly depends on its genetics and the conditions under which it lives. We have seen the importance of proper care and social conditions for guinea pigs. Guinea pigs are susceptible to stress, and poor husbandry and improper treatment shorten their life drastically. My animals lived to be nine to ten years old on average. They certainly wouldn't have lived that long in the wild, because in the final month they showed definite signs of aging and would have quickly been taken by predators.

Behavior: My elderly guinea pigs moved around less and were slower. Their curiosity declined noticeably. The little critters became quieter. They purred, gurgled, and called less.

Outward changes: The animals also change outwardly. Their coat becomes duller and they lose more hair. I have never noticed gray hair in my guinea pigs like that I've seen in dogs. Their eyes become cloudy and lose fluid. Pressure inside the eye changes because of this fluid loss, which probably means they don't see as well as they used to. Their immune system is affected and gradually deteriorates, making them more susceptible to diseases and parasites like fleas and mites.

Something to consider: At this stage, the guinea pig needs special care. Make sure that your senior citizen gets adequate amounts of vitamins and minerals. Otherwise, the menu stays the same. Don't overtax the animal and don't expose her to unnecessary stress, for instance by separating her from the group. At this point, the familiar routine is best for the animal. Fortunately, old animals are tolerated by the other members of the herd and are at no disadvantage. Even at mealtimes the young ones don't shove the old ones aside. Surprisingly, old animals are still mentally fit and can even learn and remember new things. Naturally, the aging process runs its course differently in every animal, but as a rule it begins late and then progresses quickly.

How Animals Learn Best

TIPS FROM
GUINEA PIG EXPERT
Immanuel Birmelin

PRACTICE TIME: Teaching your guinea pig is fun for both you and your pet. The "lesson" shouldn't last longer than 15 minutes, though.

HOW OFTEN?: Practice with the animal twice a day, with a lengthy recess between sessions.

A LITTLE HUNGER: Your pets will learn best if they are neither too hungry nor too full. If an animal is too hungry, she will be more nervous and impatient.

LOCATION: Train your guinea pig in familiar surroundings. Complete silence frightens the animal, and shrill noises will make her panic. Act the way you always do.

NO PUNISHMENT: Punishing an animal is forbidden. Punishment doesn't get results; it just causes anxiety. The guinea pigs must learn because they enjoy it. You can motivate them with a tasty reward.

DAILY RHYTHM: Periods of rest alternate with periods of activity. Guinea pigs find it difficult or impossible to learn during their rest periods.

Index

Information

Addresses

Associations and Clubs
> American Cavy Breeders
Association
16540 Hogan Avenue
Hastings, MN 55033
www.acbaonline.com
> American Rabbit Breeders
Association
(national organization for domestic
rabbit and cavy breeders)
P.O. Box 426
Bloomington, IL 61702
www.arba.net

Important Information

> Electrical accidents: To avoid
potentially fatal electrical acci-
dents, make sure that your guinea
pigs don't chew on electrical
wires.

> Allergies: Anyone who is
allergic to pet hair should be sure
to consult a physician before
getting a guinea pig.

> Danger of infection: Only a few
diseases can be transmitted to
people. Let your physician know
about your contact with animals.

> Sick animals: These should be
treated by a veterinarian.

Books

> Birmelin, Immanuel. 2007. *My
Guinea Pig*. Hauppauge, NY:
Barron's Educational Series, Inc.
> Vanderlip, Sharon L., D.V.M.
2003. *The Guinea Pig Handbook*.
Hauppauge, NY: Barron's
Educational Series, Inc.
> Kahn, Cynthia M., ed. 2007.
*The Merck/Merial Manual for Pet
Health*, Home Edition. Whitehouse
Station, NJ: Mercy & Co., Inc.
> Birmelin, Immanuel. 2001. *My
Guinea Pig and Me*. Hauppauge,
NY: Barron's Educational Series, Inc.

Other books on guinea pigs
published by Barron's:
> Behrend, Katrin. 1998. *Guinea
Pigs (A Complete Pet Owner's
Manual)*. Hauppauge, NY: Barron's
Educational Series, Inc.
> Behrend, Katrin. 1997. *The Guinea
Pig*. Hauppauge, NY: Barron's
Educational Series, Inc.

Magazines

> *Critters USA*
P.O. Box 6050
Mission Viejo, CA 92690
www.animalnetwork.com

Useful Web Sites

These contain information on care,
housing, health, poisonous plants,
pet sitters, and links to other
guinea pig sites.
> "Cavy Spirit"
www.cavyspirit.com
> "Cavy Care Site"
*www.geocities.com/Heartland/
Plains/2517*
> "Seagull's Guinea Pig
Compendium"
*www.aracnet.com/~seagull/
Guineas/*

Information on medical care:
> "Free Animal Health Resources
from the College of Veterinary
Medicine at Cornell University"
*www.vet.cornell.edu/library/
freeresources.htm*
> "Guinea Lynx: A Medical and Care
Guide for Your Guinea Pig"
www.guinealynx.com
> "VeterinaryPartner"
(information on health care)
www.veterinarypartner.com

Information on poisonous plants:
> "Cornell University Poisonous
Plants Informational Database"
*www.ansci.cornell.edu/plants/
index.html*
> "Poisonous Plants"
(University of Pennsylvania School
of Veterinary Medicine)
http://cal.vet.upenn.edu/poison

Information on pet sitters:
> "National Association of
Professional Pet Sitters"
www.petsitters.org
> "Pet Sitters International"
www.petsit.com

The Author

Dr. Immanuel Birmelin is a behavioral biologist. He has spent the past 25 years studying the behavior of pets as well as zoo and circus animals. In addition, he is a scientific adviser for wildlife films and an expert on animal husbandry. Immanuel Birmelin keeps guinea pigs, parakeets, and dogs.

The Photographer

Oliver Giel specializes in nature and animal photography. Along with his partner, Eva Scherer, he produces photographs for books, magazines, calendars, and advertisements. Learn more about his photo studio at *www.tierfotograf.com*. All photos in this book are Oliver Giel's with the exception of Ulrike Schanz: pages 18 top, 18 bottom left, 19 center left, 19 center right and Shutterstock: front cover photo.

English translation by Mary D. Lynch

All inquiries should be addressed to:
Barron's Educational Series, Inc.
250 Wireless Blvd.
Hauppauge, NY 11788
www.barronseduc.com

ISBN-10: 0-7641-3894-4
ISBN-13: 978-0-7641-3894-2

Library of Congress Catalog No.: 2008004473

Library of Congress Cataloging-in-Publication Data
Birmelin, I. (Immanuel)
   Guinea pigs / author, Immanuel Birmelin; photographer, Olver Giel. — 1st ed. for the U.S.
      p. cm.
   Includes index.
   ISBN-13: 978-0-7641-3894-2
   ISBN-10: 0-7641-3894-4
   1. Guinea pigs as pets. I. Title.

   SF459.G9B554 2008
   636.935'92—dc22   2008004473

Printed and bound in China
9 8 7 6 5

SOS – What Should I Do?

Weight gain

Problem: My adult guinea pig is gaining weight by the week. **This might help:** Check the husbandry conditions. Is the cage too small? Is the animal getting too little exercise? Is the calorie intake too high? If this isn't the case, then the only remedy is a trip to the veterinarian.

Escaped

Problem: The guinea pig has escaped from his enclosure. He is probably frightened and doesn't dare leave his hiding place. **This might help:** He will be less afraid if he hears other guinea pigs. Go out in the yard and every few minutes play a tape recording of the herd's "chattering."

Overgrown toenails

Problem: The guinea pig's nails get caught because they are too long. **This might help:** Indoors and in the outdoor enclosure, give the guinea pig a hard surface to walk on, such as tiles or paving stones. Have your veterinarian show you how to trim the nails.

Nutritional Deficiency

Problem: One of my guinea pigs had two pups, but the mother won't allow her youngsters to nurse. **This might help:** This is not a serious problem for guinea pigs, and in a pinch the youngsters can make it on their own (page 36). However, it is better to give them a milk replacer. I would recommend the following mixture: 25 ounces (700 g) cow's milk, 1-3/4 ounces (50 g) egg yolk, 5-1/4 ounces (150 g) heavy cream (30 percent butterfat), 1-3/4 ounces (50 g) sunflower oil, 3/4 ounce (20 g) vitamin-and-mineral mixture, and some vitamin C. Give the babies about 3/16 to 3/4 ounce (5 to 20 g) of the mixture per animal two to three times a day, depending on how hungry they are. You can freeze the rest in individual servings. Before feeding, warm it to body temperature.

Conflict in the cage

Problem: Recently our two male guinea pigs started biting each other, although they have been living together for several years and always got along well until now. **This might help:** Usually the only remedy is to castrate one of the two adversaries. If even that doesn't help, both animals must be castrated.